This Strange Garment

Also by Nicole Callihan

Books

Translucence (with Samar Abdel Jaber)

SuperLoop

Chapbooks

Elsewhere (with Zoë Ryder White)

Downtown

The Deeply Flawed Human

A Study in Spring (with Zoë Ryder White)

Novella

The Couples

This Strange Garment

Nicole Callihan

Terrapin Books

Terrapin Books
4 Midvale Avenue
West Caldwell, NJ 07006

www.terrapinbooks.com

ISBN: 978-1-947896-61-1
Library of Congress Control Number: 2022947724

First Edition

Cover art by Anne Pollard James
Pretty Mouth
16 x 20, oil on canvas

Cover design by Diane Lockward

for Eva and Ella

Contents

IV.

V.

It was once suggested to me that, as an antidote to crying, I put my head in a paper bag.

—*Joan Didion*

Where is the serene length, it is there and a dark place is not a dark place, only a white and red are black, only a yellow and green are blue, a pink is scarlet, a bow is every color. A line distinguishes it. A line just distinguishes it.

—Gertrude Stein

Everything Is Temporary

If I were faceup in the MRI machine, I'd see the cherry blossoms affixed to the ceiling.

But I'm facedown.

My arms are extended above my head.

A crane, I read this morning, can stay aloft for up to ten hours.

It barely needs to flap its wings.

There is a plastic window and a mirror to make me feel as if I can see the women on the other side of the glass.

If I'm scared, I should squeeze the egg.

I'm scared, but I don't squeeze the egg.

Everything is temporary, I say in my head.

Everything is temporary, I say over and over.

This makes me feel better.

Everything is temporary.

Until it makes me feel worse.

Everything is temporary.

But feeling worse feels foolish, because really, *Everything is temporary.*

On the way to the hospital, I dropped two letters into the blue mailbox.

Now, on a train headed north, the chatty lady across the aisle is also drinking a White Claw. She takes off her mask to show me how friendly she is.

I have breast cancer, I say, *and really don't want to deal with Covid during my surgery.*

Everything is temporary.

Even my friendship with this lady across the aisle. Even though we both drink White Claw and have paid for a Business Class ticket.

Cranes are perennially monogamous.

I'm not sure what this means, but Wikipedia tells me it's important, that scientists study it.

If early mating attempts fail, they will divorce.

Everything is temporary.

I suppose a failure for cranes is simply something that doesn't result in an egg which won't result in a bird which won't result in 20-30 years of flight.

Are you okay? The woman behind the glass asks.

I don't think so, I say. *Can I move?*

No, she says.

I wiggle my toes inside my doubled up socks. She says nothing. I have moved, undiscovered. It's like being naked under your coat.

This morning, after teaching, before heading to the hospital, I stood in my panties in front of the mirror.

I thought, *this is my temporary body.*

I've been having dreams in which I am only a body.

Zoë dreamed she could unzip her body from herself, but I dreamed there was no self.

What if Zoë were to help me out of my dress some evening, like I used to zip or unzip my mother?

Come, mother would say, *zip me up*.

Or, returning home, *Come unzip me.*

But in the evening light, Zoë, having rubbed a little egg-shaped soap to my zipper's metal teeth, would discover my absence. *Oh goodness*, she might say, *There is nothing here,* and then, because she is kind, *But you are fine just the way you are.*

The train attendant wears a glitter mask, and the man in front of me has made several calls that begin, *Hey, honey.* Is he calling the same *honey* every time? Does he call everyone *honey?*

If stored properly, honey stays good for decades.

But how does one know what has been properly stored?

Today is the thirteenth anniversary of my wedding; it is the seventh month of the pandemic; it has been three and a half weeks since I found out I have cancer; the election is in fourteen days.

Everything is temporary.

Even the patriarchy, and my White Claw, and the crane's flight, and the machine still beeping in my brain, the pretty red mesh of the bandage where the IV was inserted, the clouds crossing the train's window, the train, the window, even the beautiful expanse of river that has finally opened to me, the changing leaves, the reflection of the changing leaves in the river of the changed leaves, the sky, even the searching, the reaching, the naming, even those. Even this, *temporary.*

I.

A Different August

I think *weathered oak* for the floors,
but my husband leans toward *fruitwood.*
He has a better eye than I do.
Midsummer, and my wants aren't many.
I pay the bills, pick up the car from the shop,
send my daughter YouTube videos
on *how to insert a tampon*. Yesterday, I made
white beans and kale, tomatoes, fish.
I weeded for hours. The doctor says the lumps
aren't cancer; they are milk crystallizing—
fallen stars, after so many years. Settling.
Like salt at the bottom of a glass of water. I pour
cream in a bowl for a cat I don't have.
Maybe I'll lap it up with my tongue,
become something other than I've already become.

Imaging

blue cloth gown/ washed so often/ and at such high temperatures/
as to become/ the softest thing/ that has ever touched/ my body/ I
want to lie down/ on the cold tiles/ pull the gown over my head/
over my mother's head/ grandmother's/ the radiologist Galena's
head/ she touches me/ with such kindness/ and intelligence/ that I
want to kiss her/ but instead I cry/ and thank her/ she says
something in Russian/ and then says it's her job/ and I wonder if I
might ever/ do my job so well/ I think about the surgery/ I think/
I want them/ to take both of my breasts/ just take them/ leave
long scars/ I will be/ a different woman/ more blue cloth/ bendy
straw/ that ice for a while/ then out on the street/ no better/ just
more me maybe/ no shame/ no stretch at the buttons/ no my
eyes/ are up here/ look me/ in my eyes/ I'm alive/ look me/ in my
eyes/ I'm/ Galena tells me to breathe/ Breathe, honey, she says/
Galena tells me to hold my breath/ now breathe/ now hold it
again/ now fold your arm/ like a wing/ now look this way/
pretend the door/ is a window/ and you're looking through it/ and
what you see/ is not beautiful/ but is what is

More Like Wings

It wasn't an illness as much as it was a grouping of blackbirds on a telephone wire, or at least that's what the doctor said. She asked me to stick my tongue out farther. She said, this is a pale tongue, indicating your poor diet. She asked me what I had been feeding myself, if I ate crows, etc. I told her about the handful of almonds, the coffee. She asked me to lift up my arms. Like this? I asked. No, she said. More like wings. I made my arms into wings. Also, I scratched at my scalp. She explained this was a consequence of being around children too much and too often. They are dirty, she said. But I love my children, I told her. I am not here to talk about love, she said. While my arms were out it occurred to me that I missed the physical world, that if I were to rid myself of anything, I did not want to drag it and drop it into some "pretend" trash can, I wanted to burn it, or shred it, or fashion it into huge paper wings, hurl it off a very high building, and see if it could fly. You can put your arms down, the doctor said. But I couldn't. I could only lower them a tiny bit, then lift, then lower, and lift and lower. In this way, I experienced flight for the first time. I found my kin along the telephone wire. From my throat, I released one final call, but the doctor, having perhaps been distracted by her own longings, had already dismissed herself from our virtual appointment.

At Lost Lake

The hands are not stopped at noon,
are pouring clean water from a green pitcher.
The vacancy in me flashing from the road.
Swimming pool. CABLE TV. Park in back.
The motor inn and the two-hearted ale.
The dragonfly. This afternoon, my friends
have bare feet and the frogs are fighting.
It is not lost on us that we will each die.
One and then the other. Organs hardening.
I will make myself soft. I will own myself.
I will watch the shadow of these leaves
until the clouds come, and then, I will wait
for their shape to return. O inlet. O cove.

Caitlin rows us to the middle of the lake,
her slight, strong shoulders. We sit in sun
until we grow thirsty. Zoë has baked a cake
for my forty-sixth birthday. Will we sing?
We are already singing. What's surrendered?
Which road did we ride in on and which out?

A black band on a straw hat. A green fly
on the blue cheese. It's August, again. The ache.
The downpour. To be out of your head, out
of your element, out in the elements, elemental.
In and out and without and with and with and with.
If a day is to eternity as eternity is to a day.
If evening. If when. Zoë says she's grown brave

about picking up the parts of dead rodents.
And we have all grown brave, haven't we?
Brave and undignified. The end of summer
collecting like sweat on the backs of our thighs.

Dear Doctor—

Spring came,
is here.
Was here.

Now gone.
Learned the names
of flowers.

Made bread.
Can't come.
Now, summer.

Sideways rain.
Six months
turns nine

turns twelve.
My girl, eleven.
The other, eight.

Date night
at the dump.
Moon wanes.

Still summer.
Now gone.
Was here.

Now, fall.
Dear doctor—
must follow up

on follow-up.
On follow-up
must follow up.

Dear doctor.
Moon waxes.
Dear doctor.

What now?

Within Reach

The storm moves towards the house.
How many miles between the sound and the light.
What is the trick for not getting struck?

To stand in the storm like our ancestors.
How time moves through us like a current.
How the current moves through us like a wave.

How I am unmoved at the dark of the window.
All things are insufficient.
Our bodies are animals, and will be.

I come with little to offer. A rod.
The tree's trunk splays and parts.
Says, Touch me.

In the far kitchen, a man with pistachios and a bottle of coke.
At the bend, boiled peanuts in a brown bag.
Without proper grounding, we burn.

I dare you to look away. Double dog. Triple.
The stark shadow I make of you.
The rumbling, deep and far, and close.

So close. O storm, you are within.

The Call

And yet, there's always
the *and yet*—the fish slips
through the silver net,

the strands of hair
that fall and fall
from the fastened

gold of your barrette.
And yet, and yet—
this weather's wrong,

the words will come
from a different song:
a number unfamiliar.

The voice that rings—
and blares and thrums—
distinctly through your body.

The Kaffeeklatsch

For a short time, I was in a kaffeeklatsch, a group of Brooklyn mothers, all of P.S. 29 second grade girls who palled around with their braids and their Girl Scout uniforms and, on Fridays, went to gymnastics in Manhattan. Manhattan! These girls and their mothers and I and my girl would take the A-train to Chambers Street, the girls playing souped-up versions of patty-cake, the mothers complaining about the girls or the husbands or the jobs they had left for the husbands and the girls. Quite religiously we'd meet at the little coffee shop on the corner of Warren and Court, and every time we'd meet, I'd empty two packets of Sweet'n Low into my Matcha Green Tea, and I'd have this nearly imperceptible fantasy while stirring the Sweet'n Low into the Matcha that I would cause an explosion, that our little corner of Brooklyn would suddenly burst into flames, that I'd have to watch, first, the invisible makeup melt off, then the skin of the faces, the skin around the neck, clavicle, bones of the arms, and one day, I said, *Sometimes, I worry my Sweet'n Low Matcha will cause an explosion*. Someone laughed, said, *No, but it* will *give you cancer*, which is why I bring it up now. One of the lesser discussed aspects of having cancer is imagining all the poor choices you made which contributed to it: there are the cigarettes, of course, cliché!, all that wine, also cliché!, but then there is the Tab my mother fed me from a straw, the vats of French onion dip that held me over during the first one hundred days of isolation, huge bites of orange mac and cheese I still take from my daughters' plates, fish sticks, unwashed lettuce, pears absently devoured without even cleaning the skin on my blue jeans, even the air, just walking around breathing the air, sucking it in, and stress, how people say, *You've always been quite hard on yourself*, the very Virgo-ness, every little packet you have ever ripped open anticipating the end of the world and finding, well, finding what you find.

November Corollary

It's sleeting.

In an hour, I'll drive an hour west.

Zoë will meet me with her nit comb and a coconut cake.

We'll spend an hour, and then I'll drive an hour east.

Have I gotten what I deserved?

The sleet might turn to rain.

Might turn to snow; might stop.

There could be lice; there could be nothing.

Her comb may come out clean.

The knife.

What is it that I deserve? Clarity? Pain?

This cold wind.

Affordable health care.

Some measure of shame.

At the ballot box, I read the instructions carefully.

As if I do not know how to fill in bubbles.

And then, at the pharmacy, waiting for medication, I browse the greeting cards.

As if I might send you a greeting card.

A whale, an elephant, a happy birthday, hope it is grand.

I throw away half my breakfast.

As if there are not hungry children.

Thumb these words on my phone.

As if my fingers are not numb from cold.

Is this what I deserve?

What is it you tell yourself when offering me your sympathy?

That you are relieved you never picked up my bad habits.

A metal crane on the weather vane.

I salute your righteousness.

The S of south.

The sound of what falls.

It has not always been this way.

Summer collected. Now, this crunch of leaves.

These crumbs already down my blouse.

I've been thinking about how one never knows how the cake turns out until one has the cake.

There is no tense in Mandarin, my students tell me.

I walk.

Yesterday, I walk. Tomorrow, I walk.

Same love.

Just, I love.

Yesterday, I love. Tomorrow.

Bird flies. Sleet falls.

Even though it has stopped.

I drive. East. West.

As if, a state of being.

Consequent. Resultant.

My just dessert.

Sunday Morning

There was the god
that was in the peaches
in the cobbler, and the god
in the rosebuds in the glasses
on the table where the chicken,
fried, swam in the syrup
from the waffles, and the god
in the sweet tea, and the god
of my daughters laughing, the god
of all the women opening their blouses,
all the women saying, you'll be okay, honey,
and the god in the scars,
and the god in what got cut out,
or what would soon get cut out,
and the god of the sun
on my face, while the breeze,
was god, yes, *my god*, the breeze.

II.

The Long Ride Home

Mother and I take a black car from uptown to Brooklyn. There are sirens and rain. At home, I will sketch pictures of birds onto a large silk sheet, though I do not know how to sketch and have forgotten the curvature of birds. This one has large wings. My friend sent pink cloth to make the body. On the bumps, I hold my breath, and the driver, looking in his rearview mirror asks if I'm okay, says I'll be okay. There is an okayness in the world, yes, even though the color of fresh blood is startling. I say, *Even the weather is okay today*, and the driver agrees. He is an ornithologist, he tells me. Mother stares out the window: a flock of dreams grazing in the cemetery. *That must be interesting*, I say. *It is interesting*, he says, *if you like birds*. I do not want to laugh because it hurts to laugh, and also I don't know if the driver means to be funny. If you are tide-curious, it is interesting to visit the museum of the moon. If eros is obsolete, it is interesting to cover your body in flowers, to place lady slipper orchids where your flesh used to be, china berries up your nostrils, tree peonies in the soft space of your open legs. Already, I'm intoxicated, ill, at ease. *Wake up*, mom says. A hallucinatory citadel, a locked door. *You're home.*

Out Past the Sugar Maple

Though I can no longer feel
my breasts, I am so gentle with them,
as if a beloved dog, dead—
how tender you were when you carried her
to the cleared space beneath the trees.

The Shadows

The cross section of a shadow is a two-dimensional silhouette.

If I hold up my hand, say.

Or, sleeping on my mother's lap in the days before days.

The cotangent of the sun's elevation angle.

Like sitting on the stairs, like sirens.

A cashmere scarf at the throat, a neatly folded sail.

If I made a list of my fears, it would begin this way.

The loss of light moves at the speed of light.

A list of all I desire would begin similarly.

This property allows for the sky to appear blue.

Once, I walked in darkness, found you, walked away.

Gradually, things begin to blur.

The light pattern goes to shadow diamonds to undifferentiated
black areas.

In an acoustic shadow, I can't hear the dog barking.

The warping of a life.

The dreaming of a dream in which one dreams of dreaming.

By which I mean: *I'm still here.*

The Winter Bees

What kills cancer in a dish
or a mouse may not kill cancer
in a woman. Dishes and mice.
Wishes and rice. In such
that laboratory compounds
are best suited to laboratories.
But what of this room? This body?
It's early fall. The soft sun. Outside,
the children laugh. Somewhere not far,
a cluster of figures surrounds wax combs.
The winter bees will soon be born.
What is replaced is not irreplaceable.

Woman with Bright Spots

Vlad, my radiologist, assures me I will feel nothing. *Only happiness*,
he says.

Hungry, I stare out the window. He slaps the inside of my elbow,
tells me he has rarely seen such beautiful veins.

This pleases me. Even now, I'm a sucker for beauty.

I take a deep breath, look away, feel something, barely.

Is *this* happiness? Pinch me.

The sugar water attached to a radioactive isotope moves through
my veins.

Maybe after I'll get a steak from Smith & Wollensky's, a wedge salad.

Or, a grilled swiss with bacon and tomato on rye plus Funyuns
from the deli.

I will take picture of your insides, Vlad says. *Like Picasso!*

I imagine myself Picasso's Weeping Woman. My blue teeth
chattering, red bow, canary yellow ear, the fear.

The machine will read for bright spots.

Cancer being the brightest of spots.

There are stars. All light is information. Or is it the other way around?

Before surgery, I met Zoë and Caitlin at the cabin and Zoë brought us jars of moonwater. You just leave the jar outside on a full moon then drink it up. It'll make you live forever. Or want to. We drank some of it, saved the rest.

This, too, is a stage of survival.

Hoarder of light and color. Woman in an Armchair. Woman with a Flower. Woman Throwing a Stone. Girl Before Mirror. Interior with Girl. Woman by the Window. Woman at the Mouth of a Machine.

Vlad asks me to lift my arms.

I can't, I say. *Only this high*, I say, which is not very high. The scars aren't even really scars yet, still just wounds.

And so Vlad tucks my hands beneath my hips.

Now, I'm a botched painting, but then, I held the jar of moonwater to my chest and felt the glass vibrate with my heart's hard pumping.

Was *that* happiness?

Vlad puts two blankets over my body. A chill I can't shake. Last week, at home, recovering in bed, I asked Kristin to cover my face with the long cashmere shawl I've been sleeping with. *This isn't funny*, she said. But did it anyway. And we laughed. Until it hurt.

In the machine, I dream for a minute. I sleep. I panic, breathe, sleep again, startle, breathe. I can feel the weight of the waves on my face, the ripple across my shoulders, my sore sternum.

When I checked in, Sandra, at the desk told me she has known my oncologist for forever. *Fifteen years!* She said.

Forever. And a day. Forever and ever. Forever, or fifteen years, whichever comes first.

I'm in the machine *forever*. And then I'm out.

Now, we can start test, Vlad says. But he is joking. He wraps a bright blue cloth around my arm from where the IV went in. It is an exquisite blue, a blue I've witnessed only a handful of times, a blue I could count on my fingers.

And then, I am Woman in Changing Room Removing Gown. Woman Not Looking at Mirror. Woman Fastening Surgical Bra. Woman in Sweater, in soft pants, in Elevator. Woman Under Broken Sky Shoving Broken Pretzels from Dented Ziploc Baggie Fished from Bottom of Woman's Bag in Woman's Tired Face.

I am Woman Not Weeping on Street Corner, Not Weeping in Cold New York Air, Not Weeping on the Long Ride Home, Not Weeping Woman.

O woman, don't weep.

Breathing Lessons

I have been practicing holding
my breath. The radiologist says

if I can hold it for forty seconds,
everything will be easier, so here,

writing this sentence, I hold
my breath as long as I can; I even

punctuate with a semicolon so I
may hold my breath longer. It occurs

to me that this might give me more
months, more years, more decades,

which would make many things easier,
though not aging, or retirement money,

unrequited love, or remembering.
As you get older, memory starts taking

the shape of a childhood television show.
The fuzz and bunny ears. The snow.

Your brother taunts you; your mother runs
bathwater; your father, in another house,

stirs his other children's macaroni.
I think if I can get really good at this I'll

swim more in the coming summers.
The blue pool. Swan dive. Butterfly.

A sort of drowning without drowning.

Amazon

To get through what promises to be a long winter, I've purchased a UV lamp.

It's about the size of a small dinner plate and weighs a little more than a pound.

Because I have Prime, it arrived in one day.

On a Wednesday, in the half dark of noon—still in my flowered robe, still with tubes draining fluid from my body—I thought I'd die, or want to so much that I might as well die, before again seeing a crocus push from the earth. By Thursday, I was bathed in light.

Artificial light, electric light, but light.

Of course, I'm not without shame.

The cardboard boxes stacked and tied in the pantry.

And the other cardboard boxes that arrive and arrive.

Juven to mix into water for wound healing; a new dry brush; the machine to project stars on Eva's ceiling because there's a pandemic and I have cancer so she should have stars on her ceiling if she wants them; the protein bars and macadamia nuts; one of those triangle Calvin Klein bras for if I ever don't need the sad, pink bra the hospital provided; another machine to project stars on Ella's ceiling because Eva has stars on hers and there's a pandemic and I have cancer so Ella should have stars too if she wants them.

Artificial, electric, but stars.

And another box to break down.

Amazon.

A, meaning "without" plus *mazos*, variant of *mastos*, "breast," meaning *without breast;* meaning *without breast.*

Woman without breasts.

Woman without breasts but with many boxes.

Woman without breasts but with many boxes which will arrive in one day.

Prime woman. Woman in prime. Or, woman who while in Prime
paid for Prime and so even after Prime does not cancel Prime because
woman wants light.

Who can so easily give up light?

The Amazons cut or burned off one breast so they could draw bowstrings more efficiently.

But I can hardly throw a ball, and I let the doctors do it.

I followed my doctor, a pretty woman with five-year-old triplets,
a woman who wears gorgeous, expensive high heels, but who for
surgery was clogged and masked, into the operating room. I said,
It is so weird to walk myself into the operating room.

Everything was bright.

The anesthesiologist gave me a thumbs up, and I said something like, *Whoa science is cool*, and when I woke up in ICU, the light was dim and the machines were beeping, and I was underneath a plastic blanket filled with hot air.

For a while, I pretended I was on the beach. My friend came to sit on the blanket we'd laid out, and for a long time we stared straight into the sun, and then, when it got too hot, we took off our clothes and swam in the sea.

But then the drugs wore off.

For anesthesia, the Amazons likely used powdered opium in a cup of wine.

Or, nothing.

The former sounds rather delicious and appealing; something I might *add to my cart* or *buy now*; something that might be *arriving tomorrow*; something I might feel a twinge of shame about as I take a knife and cut into the seam of the box, surprised at how easily it collapses.

How easily it collapses. All of it. The body, its counterparts.

Like tripping on the cord to your new lamp, how the darkness comes as quickly as the light.

How the light—if I can get down on my knees and find the outlet—might come again.

A Fog

I have been moving in and out of one.
Every few hours, I hold my hand up
to my face. If I can see the hand,
I move towards the window; if I can't,
I stay in bed. Usually, the fog is caused
by an absence of wind. One winter,
in Chicago, I walked until my fingers
were raw. That night, in a motel room,
I rubbed ChapStick into the bloody spots
of my knuckles. Months later, in Oklahoma,
a heat spell blistered my shoulders.

It's not that I need to see. There are walls
to run the hands along. The fret. The rolling.
The body is strange matter. This mass of me.
How moist the land. Scientists measure
the fog on the order of tens of centimeters.

When mother and I lived in South Dakota
we were so far from the grocery store we packed
our things on dry ice. A hunk of meat, some milk.
Mornings, before the sun came up, we played
cards. 6 of Spades. Jack. Heart. That far north,
the sun rises late. When we finally got home,
we'd pour water over what was left
in the brown paper sack. I'd pretend I was
disappearing. Was I? I didn't yet know
much about bodies. Now, though, if I hold

my breath long enough, I can feel
my solar plexus pulsing. It pulses so hard,
I think I might drown. But I don't.

The Extravagant Stars

Everybody says the stars are dead.

By the time the light reaches us—

As if the light itself is not enough—

Or maybe everybody says most stars are dead? Or some of the people say all the stars are dead, and all the people say some of the stars are dead.

Is the sun dead?

I don't know. I can't remember.

1 in 2 women can't remember 1 in 2 things.

I have all these *facts* in my *head.*

These *claims* about the *world.*

Caterpillars, supernovas, the days getting shorter, longer again.

The riverbed. Our great confluence.

The buzz of *that* particular fly.

Did you ever get my postcard from Mexico?

I write the same word over and over, and mostly that word is *light.*

I keep saying, *It seems very unlikely that this will kill me.*

But why unlikely?

Medically speaking, you have a 1 in 500 chance of being born
with 11 fingers or toes.

I had a student once without thumbs.

I wanted him to write a poem about it.

He used his hands like lobster claws; he made me so sad. Or I
was so sad, and he reminded me of my sadness.

He didn't want to write about his thumbs, he said.

Probably he wrote about outer space.

Some years later, I had a terrible late-term miscarriage and had
to go to a terrible late-term abortion clinic with terrible, terrible lighting.
Afterwards, they gave me a root beer-flavored lollipop.
I sat in a blue chair and sucked on my lollipop. I was a little girl
and an old woman. I cried audibly. I was in my *prime*.

1 in 4 women will *this*. 1 in 8 women will *that*. 1 in 15 women
will *thisandthat*.

And yet, the death rate of stars is only one about every 10,000
years or so.

Meaning, the naked eye will probably never see a dead star. You're looking
into the past, yes, but it's unlikely, though not impossible,
that you're seeing a dead star.

Looking into the past is like sticking your thumb in the dirt of the Dixie Cup.

But a high-powered telescope changes everything.

I think what I'm saying is: I'd rather live than not live.

When I was writing about my terrible late-term miscarriage, I gave a reading on the Upper East Side.

Several women came up to me to tell me I was brave. *So brave,* they said.

I didn't want to be brave; I wanted to be brilliant.

In hindsight, this strikes me as incredibly dim-witted.

1 in 1 woman will look back on something and feel foolish.

Now, I will take brave any day.

I will take brave and fold it into my little kerchief and tie it to my stick and carry it to the top of the highest hill I can find, and when I get there, I'll rest my tired legs, unwrap my little hunk of pie from its wax paper, and stare up at the brilliant, extravagant stars, knowing that they are not dead, not even one of them, not dead at all, but living, pulsing, pressing their light as far as it can reach.

III.

The As If Of

I haven't yet mentioned that they moved my belly button.

Actually they didn't move it; they took it off and moved
everything around it, and then they sewed it back into the exact
spot I'd point to if someone were to ask where my belly button is.

Like asking a toddler where her ears are, her mouth, her face.

Like stealing her nose. The rose of your thumb between
your fingers.

Like asking the dog where her bone is.

Though no one asks where my belly button is.

I wonder why it wasn't tossed with the other scraps.

In this way, just after the solstice, most everything began
feeling arbitrary.

The ice cubes flushed down the toilet, a spoon stuck under
a pillow.

Mama Heaton's gall bladder in a pink plastic bucket; that kid
from seventh grade's spleen.

The buttermilk poured on my stepmother's bread.

The alphabet, the weather, the yellow stars scratched into your skin.

That paper donkey with so many tails where a tail shouldn't be.

I'm not sure what to say about the balloons tangled in the gumball tree.

The fibrous forest. Another vial of drawn blood.

I doubt I could pick my body from a lineup.

For weeks, I felt like I was dragging a sour dish towel beneath
my brain.

That one, I'd say to the lineup officer, the one with the lemons,
the one that reeks of this morning's milk, last night's lamb juice,
the raw food I sneak to the dog.

In the beginning, there was a body.

Also, the fear of never being desired again, of never desiring, of
saying desire so many times it becomes *dire*.

Then, the incinerated parts, the parts that washed down the drain,
the parts that were useless but still salvaged, the parts that no
longer served any use.

If you say belly button over and over, it'll start to sound like
something else. Like saying *hydrangea* until it becomes a bomb.

The Alternative

Having woken in my own hot arms,
my own hot body clinging to the sheets,
and the sweat of me, and the snow
beyond the snow, beyond the snow
out the window, I strip naked,
lie on the marble, let the cool of it
move to my bones. It is something
to be on fire, my last best burning
in the winter. It is something
for the heat of a life to collect and collect
in the small of your back, the blades
of the shoulders, a kindling, a kinder
reminder. How when you were young
the women on the porch said,
It's better than the alternative, and because
you were a fool, you doubted them,
because you were a fool, you thought
beauty was whole, something to be
observed, slick as a magazine page,
to be desired like so many mouthfuls
of cake, to be revered, a cockeyed
crown, shiny, and without fear
of drowning, of going down, of depths
unknown, but now that you have
woken in your own hot arms
in a winter with its own sort of wars,
you know better. Don't you?

Equine Behavior

Ella asks if you have to be lying down to die.

I think you can die then fall, I say.

Or you can be in a seated position.

We ask Siri.

But Siri wants to talk about horses.

She says you should slap the horse.

If you can't lift the horse on your own, have someone help you lift the horse.

But you must get the horse on its feet. Walk it in circles.

Hock and fetlock.

When I could finally drive, I drove myself to the doctor, circled the block for parking.

The winter was mild. Is mild.

I still have last year's gloves balled up in the bottom of my bag.

The painful joints, the navicular bone.

Lonely, sleep-deprived horses may be resistant to schooling.

The sky is half very blue, half very grey; my husband coughs in the shower.

If you blow into a horse's nostrils, it will be dedicated to you for life.

This is true.

Or at least partially true. Like most everything.

Truth being its own sort of saddle.

To Get to the Other Side

"Do you ever feel like an alien?" I ask Cliff. He's arranging my body on the radiation table. Usually I apologize for my muddy boots, but today I am feeling more and more like my childhood alien abduction dreams were actually dreams about middle-aged cancer treatment. "Like you've taken me from a field of poppies," I say, "and are performing bizarre intergalactic experiments on me." Cliff laughs and secures my arm in the vice. He closes the twelve-inch steel door behind him. Once I'm inside the radiation tube, I'm not supposed to think about Marie Curie's cataracts or her fingernails falling off or the fact that her casket is made of lead, so instead, I repeat, over and over, *Healing Radiant Light, Healing Radiant Light,* and when I get bored of repeating *Healing Radiant Light*, I make up jokes instead. *Horse walks into a bar with a Camel hanging from his mouth. Bartender says, Need . . . A . . . Healing . . . Radiant . . . Light?* Cliff is on the other side of the glass; his voice booms through the speaker. "You ready?" He asks. I give a thumbs-up. *Why did the woman cross the road? To get to the Healing Radiant Light.* Cliff tells me to breathe in, "Deeper, Deeper, that's it," he says, "and Hold . . ." *At least I get to be the human*, I'll tell him if he comes back . . . *Healing Radiant Light . . . Knock knock . . . Healing Radiant Light . . . Who's there . . . Healing . . .* "And release," he says. I open my eyes to see the pine trees they've painted on the ceiling to trick my mind into thinking I'm lying in a field on the earth staring up through the green and into the spacious blue sky; the eye of the machine scans me, beeps, holds. "And again," Cliff says. *How many women does it take to screw in a healing radiant lightbulb?*

One.

Recovery Room 4

My body, the paper chair. I dig
for words, like fishing for a pill
in the bottom of your purse.

The crawl space dream. It's all plain
as day. My voice is gone. Dirty elbows.
The underside of the sky.

The anesthesiologist calls my name.

The skin, right now,

the doctor says, is more like paper
than skin; it can so easily tear;
someone might write their name
in pencil; drag their hand
along the graphite; wipe the smudge
on their old jeans; decide against it;
take the pink pearl from its pouch;
and rub so hard at the letters
as to make a hole; the blue lines;
the pale pulp—*be gentle, so gentle*—
to be writ on; to be shredded;
folded and hidden in a book;
fashioned into an airplane
and shot through the hallway of sky.

IV.

Humiliation

Traced back to the Latin *humus*, meaning, "earth, ground."

As in, my dirty hands.

Giving rise to the verb *humiliare.*

In the first two stories, there were peonies, but in the third, a girl
in a bloody coat.

The doctor says, I might expect my voice to lower.

Hair thinning is not unusual.

Last summer, I took a photo of a tree in which it looked as if legs
were parted.

Open. Wanting. To be split.

From the Latin *furca*, meaning "fork."

I also took a photo of a drawer of spoons. My many upside-down faces.

Bifurcate. May constipate.

Loss of appetite.

And I was just starting to get hungry.

Weakness. Sleeplessness.

To dream of a lion may indicate power; may aggression; may
hunt/ hunted/ hunter.

Related to *hentan*, "to seize." Proto-germanic.

To be taken at the same time each day. Taken.

Verb (used with object).

To get into one's hold by voluntary action.

From the late Old English, *tacan*, "get (especially by force)."

Of unknown ultimate origin.

Cavity

One of the places to carry grief is in the mouth.
A recess, tongued hole, memory of the eaten.
To be filled with composite, metal, ceramic.
Not to be held as a memorized passage is held.
Or a lie. Your tongue. A drink. Crushed petals.
A title. Victor. Sinner. Wife. A title modified:
Proud victor. Reluctant sinner. Obedient wife.
I think I would rather be brainy than rich,
blotted than runny, massive than illumined.
Who is responsible for the numbing and drilling?
I am. And the masks and the gloves? I am.
The mirror, too. Where is the moon? Over there.
Any last words? No, no words, but thank you.

The Pain Scale

Nearly always, I was a six,
somewhere between a five and a six,

I'd say, between moderate and severe,
between tiger lily and hothouse orchid,

between learning how to sound out a word
I'd only ever read, and learning how to spell

despair, be in disrepair, what's the difference,
I asked, between pain and discomfort,

am I feeling pain that you've cut off my breasts,
that you've slit me from hip bone to hip bone

and taken skin and fat from my abdomen,
taken the tiniest blood vessels and moved them

to make these sort of breast-looking breasts, or is it
discomfort, is it discomfort, is it discomfort

that I cannot roll over onto my side, look at the birds
out the window, that someone has to help me

to the bathroom, that someone, or maybe just me,
will have to put on these disposable gloves—

bought to go grocery shopping in the early days
of the pandemic, o how we washed the plums!—

and use these gloves now to drag the shit out of me,
the shit that collects and collects from all the drugs,

is that pain, is that discomfort, is the crying
into the sink, is the nipple falling off in the shower,

or the other that was hanging on by what seemed
to be a thread, how I took my toenail clippers to it,

the wince, the flushing it down the toilet so as not
to draw rats to the trash, pain, I'd say, yes, somewhere

between a five and a six, I think, but maybe
a two or so, maybe an eight, but god, I'm ready

for a pleasure scale, and not moderate pleasure, I want
severe. Severed but raptured. Not comfort but pleasure.

Pure unadulterated pleasure. *Ten,* I want to say, *ten.*

Side Effects

Because of the medicine, my fingers easily bruise.

It's like I have little plums at the ready.

Only they hurt.

And they are not in the icebox.

Nor are they sweet and delicious.

But, yes, they're cold, and yes, I'm trying to save them.

Imagine how selective I now must be with the words I choose!

I will say the thing just to say it!

A Day at the Beach

The nurse says I'll likely feel okay, a little tired, very warm.

Like you've spent a day at the beach, she says.

But it's winter in New York.

After treatment, I eat two street tacos on a cold wet corner, walk to
Chinatown, pay cash for burn cream.

There's a nickel-sized blister on my clavicle.

When we were young, my brother liked me to peel his sunburned back.

Long sheets of dead skin.

We could waste a whole afternoon this way.

Sometimes, I sit very alone, rub my arm in pain, worried I'll die,
worried I won't.

Translucent in the light.

It's hard not to press a blister.

Thumb and pus. Sand and snow.

But no one wants an open wound.

Baby oil and iodine. The little playboy bunny sticker girls
used to stick above their bikini line, the pale beneath.

Waves. Breaking.

A bucket full of still sandy seashells.

The fishes, too. And, God. And, you.

I can't admit how many times I've abandoned those I love to walk along the shore, willfully burning my shoulders, feeling the ache of my legs, walking so far and for so long that I might reach the edge of the world.

And then, turning back, the walk always so much farther, wading into the ocean only deep enough to splash water onto my face, to pee, stare up into the sun, and walking again.

Finally, arriving. Sand on the blanket. My novel facedown.
No one realizing how far I'd gone.

The "Gfit"

—for Jennifer L. Knox

Those mornings, early in the pandemic,
when I was still a stranger to muting myself
and did not yet have a dog, did not yet
not mind picking up poop, which I thought
I'd mind but don't, but then, when I knew nothing
of what I would know, or what I now think I know,
though now it's probably mid-pandemic, even if
I'd like to believe it's the end of the pandemic,
but then it was early in the pandemic,
even though I thought maybe it was getting
towards the end of the pandemic,
and I didn't have cancer, or if I did,
I didn't know I had cancer, and I knew
fewer dead people, and had received far
fewer flowers, fewer gifts, and my children still felt
like something I could manage, or not manage,
but simply delight in, and so, oblivious, I'd walk along
the dock by the boats, hoping for a boat
with a perfect name. It's not that I was a stranger
to myself. I'd stand naked sometimes. Unanchored,
sure, but not actually disappearing. When I turned 40,
my mother sent me a birthday card which read,
Welcome to invisibility. None of the boats
had perfect names. They were called *Midas,*
or *Improbable.* One was *Last Light,* which seemed
close to perfect, but I sort of wanted it
to be called *First Light,* though that sounded like
a church song or a midwestern breakfast chain.

After the surgery, when my nipple fell off
in the shower, it washed down the drain.
Jen had written, wanted to send me something.
This was December. *Oh shit,* I wrote back,
one of my nipples just fell off. LOL. I had always
sort of taken my nipples as birthright,
had fed my children with them. Now, though, I wish
I'd done a wet t-shirt contest in Cancun.
Maybe there's still time! I'll get on my boat—
post-pandemic, post-treatment, posthaste, post-hope—
and wave at everyone on the shore. I'll leave
everything behind. You'll have to take out
binoculars to see my nipples are gone and to read,
in deep blue cursive, the misspelled name of my getaway boat.

P.O. Box 246

In a pretty, adjacent town once famed for importing the tusks of elephants to make ivory keys for pianos, I entered the square post office. I'd like a post box, please. The clerk asked me if it was for business or personal use, and I confided that it was personal, slid my exact change beneath the plexiglass, and memorized the combination. It was a beautiful box from another century, a copper-colored metal with a little glass window to peer into as I anticipated the missives sent from afar. The handwritten longings! They might be accompanied by a pressed flower or a stray feather! Signifiers among signifiers! For weeks, I drove to the P.O., listening to my heart drum in my throat, but found nothing save a reminder to vote from the city council. Then for several months, an unexpected illness and a string of blizzards took me to bed. Finally, I was able to return. *I almost didn't recognize you,* the clerk said. Empty-handed, I laughed. I had been so hollowed out by winter—my face and body—that I barely recognized myself and was moved that he, a near stranger, might recognize me at all. Music lilted from the ancient speakers, and when he asked if I wished to renew the box for another six months, I declined. Who had I thought might find me in that secret, tucked away place? And what did it mean that no one had?

There is no happiness

like the week after a toothache,
when the halo of pain fades,
and there are no longer ponies
running through your field
of vision, and you've stopped
praying, stopped bargaining,
stopped listing all you'd give,
please god, if only. If only,
please god. Then: nothing but
the absence of what defined you,
the sound of your own dumb breath.

V.

The Paper Anniversary

1

Paper gowns are not as soft as cloth gowns are not as soft
as silk   as milk   which is only soft until it sours

here in the wee hours I sulk   the bulk of my body
my thin skin   the membrane of my weak brain

after the fanfare   the hoopla   the careful decisions
sloppy incisions I write about the violets gone blue

the violence   that roses are red   that also pale yellow
hello?   it's been one year   what have I to fear?

these queer balloons   pop   pop
                                        pop

2

Paper gowns are not as soft as cloth gowns are not as soft
as dirt   this insidious hurt   and this and this and that

that and that and that   a rat on the grave of a spouse
a mouse   two mouses   so mice   so fuzzy dice

in a sky blue van   I should've been a man   and I wuz
and I wan and wane   am as sane as a sanitary

napkin adhered to your big fat beautiful forehead
bring me your dead   let them dance in my bed

let them swoon and spin and spin and tap tap
tap

3

Paper gowns are not as soft as cloth gowns are not as soft
as dust   the uncle who cussed   and threw bottles

his face of mottles   this pace of piecing   of piecemeal
quiet thrill   grown shrill   grown silent as a mole

on your spine   o you're divine   in your shame
this blame   your name is mud   in my eye   a chicken

thigh I licked   gnawed to the bone   this moan
a wishbone caught   in my pale clean throat

4

Paper gowns are not as soft as cloth gowns are not as soft
as water   as the eyelashes of my daughter

who perhaps I've disappointed   certainly anointed
the oils and creams   the comb I've mouthed a thousand times

the dreams   what a mystery this sealed vessel
this meal for worms   o how we squirm   in the face

of disaster   a vase full of asters   it's not love
I'm after   but after the after   after the aftermath

in which x approaches infinity   the serenity
see also: my affinity for pain

5

Paper gowns are not as soft as cloth gowns are not as soft
as the skin of the pear   pelt of the bear   the felt thing

the svelte and sung   wrung out to dry   draped
over the faucet just so   just so you know   I've lost

it   all   or am   losing   unloosing   a viper
candy-striper   sunbeam and swish   the unwashed

dish   the woman at the sink   is sinking   is thinking
to abandon a body is a different sort of song   welcome fright

this flight   the sonorous water   amorous lover
what a lark this dark   to couple and waft   drain

these noodles   I wonder how many times   I've said
brush your teeth   as if mattering   begins in the head

we'll all be dead   we'll all be dead   just brush your teeth
and go to bed

A Difficult Day

That the dog and my daughter both had their periods, and mine was nearing its end, just enough to believe I didn't need a tampon but to stain my panties anyway, and there was a bout of lice which I had given up on and so invited a woman I found on the internet into our home, even though we were at the height of a pandemic wave, and that we were all eating cookies, burned on the bottom, and maybe the woman had her period too. The house smelled like teenage pads with wings, and was decorated with shredded mouthfuls of bloody cotton from the strange diaper we'd try to pin on the dog, but which she ate. And that on this very night I was scheduled to read poems on Zoom with a man who says his own name in poems, like if in this poem I said, "Nicole, your dog and daughter are bleeding, and the whole house has lice." When my daughter started her period, someone said I should throw her a party, but I took her for pancakes. Of course it's embarrassing, all of it, this life. Syrup on your chin while you tell a child she's now a woman. And shortly after I tried to write a poem in the voice of Robert Browning called, "My Last Period," and I sent my "Menopause: An Index" out to several venues and was rejected, though I've stopped calling it rejection. Declined. I was declined. Yesterday morning I confessed to my other daughter, the younger one, that I had once eaten a scab, and this morning my friend sent me a picture of his healing thumb, and I responded, *Bodies are amazing.* Do I think bodies are amazing? That I nursed my daughters for years, and then had my breasts cut off, like in some kind of too perfect novel. And the dog wouldn't wear her cone once we had her spayed, so I sat with her on the couch to try to keep her from licking her wounds. When she was young, my older daughter, the one who now hasn't gotten her period in quite a while because of stress or counting too many calories, her friends were all named after blood: Scarlett, Rose, that sort of thing. My god, how lonely life can be, how, mostly, Nicole, it feels like sitting on a toilet, wiping and wiping, until you can no longer see the blood.

Something like gratitude

that my husband was never
a breast man; that I was wasted
on him, my stepfather once joked;
that the doctor can make nipples
of scar tissue, though they flatten
over time, or do not take at all;
that the lady can airbrush color
on my areolae, though she warns
against the deeper pinks, as I'm
getting older; that I'm getting older;
that there are calcium pills
to counteract the pills that leach
the calcium from my bones,
and other pills, and others,
and the cold water, too,
with which I swallow it all down.

I all but missed the magnolias

all but missed the breaking/ of the blossoms/ being so preoccupied
with/ my own brokenness/ my own breaking/ another blood
panel/ another marker/ to draw another incision/ another
incision/ to take another organ/ another organ/ no longer needed/
the sky a tilt/ and the birds/ when I was pregnant/ I walked
around/ in awe/ of all the people/ you were once inside someone/
I'd think/ and you and you/ you grew and grew/ you and you and/
you/ I'd be at the bagel shop/ racked with tenderness/ that each
body/ had grown/ now same same/ in awe/ of you and you/ and
you who just pulled/ your sweater/ over your head/ and you with
the black dog/ and you smoking the joint/ and you and you/ you
grew yes/ grow/ and too you will die/ and you will die/ and you
will die/ and you will die/ and you will die/ and you and you and/
you will die/and then/ who will sit beneath/ this tree missing/
what's already broken

Eighteen months later I find a tampon

in the little flower pouch I keep
in my bag, and a lighter, just in case
I start smoking again, or the oophorectomy
failed, and I'm still releasing eggs.
Now, I can tell you that Ethan Hawke
twice made eye contact with me
on the streets of Brooklyn, and so as
to spare my family from our affair,
I looked away. And popquiz!
guess who I saw read all new poems
at Bryant Park last night! It seemed
like rain, but Nick Flynn! who I also
find hot, or found hot, back when
I was more inclined to arbitrary desire.
I just kicked at the dirt and talked
to Nick about high school acceptance letters.
Where Maeve might go. Where Eva.
Didn't mention star migration,
or cancer, just started namedropping.
Oh yeah, Ada loves rose petal lattes.
Why confront the rancid, the desiccated,
the sublime when you can talk
about the weather? Which fish to release
back into the sea? My anesthesiologist
looked like Keanu Reeves w/ a beehive
and asked me to count backwards from ten.
I was all, are you wearing eyeliner, ten,
nine, eight. I was lit from within.

Seven, six, and when I woke up, five,
four, three, two. I shined—one—like
so much sun through a hospital window.

Blood Work

The phlebotomist tells me I've gotta lean into the tide.

I turn my head so as not to see the needle go in.

A habit.

Which tide to lean into?

It's the next August, what I would have called "a year from now"
  a year ago.

If a year ago was a year from now, then.

I'd like to be in the pool with Ella, holding her body to help her float, watching her bat her eyes at the sun, the sky as blue as this tourniquet.

Has it passed? Am I through?

I could spend a decade writing odes to the sound of the air conditioner.

The last time I was in this waiting room, a man in the chair beside me sketched birds. I'd hoped to see him today.

Or not him, but the birds.

Or not the birds, but the space around them.

Sky as collection of molecules above water, around bird.

What did the drowning woman say to the fish?

Kelp me.

Get it?

What's gotten. What's had. Forgotten. Forhad.

Of my to-dos, I to-did.

Of the tide, my lunitidal intervals vary.

But, really, this tourniquet is just so blue.

Being that it is late

that it is already too late,
that it was always too late,
that the day had become late,
and then the night, too, was late,
and now morning, but late
morning, but morning late
enough to be nearly noon, late
in the curve of sky, late
in my lazy walk to the train, late
with its slate roof, its roses so late
as to be dead on the vine, late
in my hunger, my hunger so late
as to have passed, my thirst late
in and of itself, water running late
down my chin, running late
into the rising river, running late
in its reflection of the stars, late
in its dipper's ladle, and I am late,
and the dream late, even the lake late,
late and frozen, but not so late
as to be frozen solid, not ice late,
but dangerous late, waterbody late,
of what the mystics call too late
for disaster, and too late, too,
for any certain heaven, snake late,
or I have again eaten my tail late,
licked clean the blue plate late,
yes, I've swallowed my fate;
stomached it. My god, it's late.

Desquamation

The room downstairs was in need of a good cleaning, but it was my room; or perhaps because it was my room, it was in need of a good cleaning. Not that I had dragged in dirt from the garden, but that I was shedding the outermost membrane of my skin. In 2011, the same year I lost one pregnancy and found my last, Charles Weschler and his colleagues explained that humans shed their entire outer layer of skin every 2-4 weeks. This seems counter to the seven years I learned in grade school when my favorite joke was *your epidermis is showing*. But yes, since I began these sentences, I've likely shed .009 ounces of skin, which doesn't sound like a lot, but line by line, it adds up, and so by the time my husband visits my downstairs room, he might drag his finger across the dust of my desk and ask how I can live this way. I am living, yes? And this way. The scientific term is desquamation, from the Latin desquamare, meaning "to scrape the scales off a fish." Each summer, comes a morning, when walking to the river, I discover a number of dead fish have washed up onto the bank, and I'm startled, a hook in my heart, and each summer, on that morning, I promise myself I will not be startled again. I will not be startled again. O dust. I am not the same woman who began this story.

This Strange Garment

Morning. Absent of sound
but for the winter wren,

the space heater. Millstone.
Fontanelle. Skein of geese.

Threat of rain. How to
sustain? Jean said that on

the anniversary of her death
we should sit in lamplight,

sing to a bowl of lemons,
praise the resonant sac.

O bladder and follicle.
Hymen and tree. The underside

of me. So purply bruised.
To what do I owe the honor

of one more cold day,
the warm script, the grit

and gloss of being? Mother
writes to say she still

can't taste. The curdled
cream. I dreamed it was

afternoon. The spirit pined
for an avenue of bodies.

An evening rush. What comes
after the after? A blouse

on a doorknob. The hush.

Acknowledgments

I am grateful to the editors of the following journals where these poems first appeared:

Anti-Heroin Chic: "The Paper Anniversary" (2, 3, and 4)

Asterix: "The Alternative," "The As if Of," "Desquamation," "The Extravagant Stars," "Woman Becoming"

Bellevue Literary Review: "Imaging"

BOMB: "Everything Is Temporary"

Booth: "There Is No Happiness"

Calyx: "The Paper Anniversary" (1 and 5)

Conduit: "Cavity," "Within Reach"

Five Points: "Being that it is late"

Gasher: "I all but missed the magnolias"

Ghost City Review: "Dear Doctor—"

Heavy Feather Review: "A Day at the Beach"

Juniper: "Sunday Morning"

Mid-American Review: "A Different August" (as "Days")

MORIA: "The Shadows"

Northern New England Review: "More Like Wings" (as "The Afterlife")

Ocean State Review: "Blood Work"

On the Seawall: "Breathing Lessons," "The 'Gfit,'"
"The Kaffeeklatsch," "The Long Ride Home"

PENN Review: "P.O. Box 246"

Rogue Agent: "The Pain Scale"

Salamander: "A Fog," "To Get to the Other Side"

SWWIM: "Something Like Gratitude"

Thrush: "Equine Behavior," "This Strange Garment"

Trampoline: "Amazon," "Humiliation," "Woman with Bright Spots"

Witness: "A Difficult Day"

Zócalo Public Square: "At Lost Lake" (as "At Blue Lake")

"The Extravagant Stars" was featured on *The Slowdown* on February 4, 2022.

Navigating illness is difficult at any time, but navigating illness during a pandemic felt especially onerous. Being able to write poems while navigating that illness was a gift. I'm so grateful for the many people in my life who made that gift possible.

To Zoë Ryder White, who reads nearly every poem I write, almost immediately, sometimes before I even write it, often alongside me, and always offering, if even metaphorically, a jar of moonwater to my parched mouth. To Kristin Dombek, my ride or die, who often, during this time, was my *actual* ride: please don't ever die. To the other dear poet and writer friends who I've loved and been inspired by for decades: Russell Carmony, Lorraine Doran, Iris Jamahl Dunkle, Caitlin McDonnell, Sanjana Nair, and Marion Wrenn. And to the ones who keep me syntactically sound, cloaked in silk robes and exquisite flowers: Stephanie Hopkins, Ada Limón, and Dawn Lundy Martin.

I'm grateful, too, to the extensive virtual communities who nourished me in this time. To Kai Coggin, whose *Wednesday Night Poetry* propelled me from week to week, poem to poem. To Angie Cruz, who welcomed me to *Asterix Journal* as Artist-in-Residence in Winter 2021, where so many of these poems first appeared. To those who inhabited the various daily or weekly spaces where I first made and shared much of this work: Denver Butson, Terence Degnan, Carol Dorf, Mara Jebsen, Rachel Neve Midbar, Lara Payne, Michael Robins, Noel Sikorski, Joanna Solfrian, Michael Tyrell, Sara Wallace, and Kathleen Winter. To the women of the Matrix who surely did a ritualistic dance around this manuscript: Michele Kotler, Brenda Cardenas, Jane Creighton, Laura Cronk, Janet Jennerjohn, Ruth Ellen Kocher, Kristin KP Peterson, Catherine Esposito Prescott, Robin Reagler, and Suzanne Wise; and to my fellow poet moms who gave me generous, detailed feedback: Emily Carlson, Kristen Hanlon, and Anna VQ Ross.

For the time and space to complete this book, I am indebted to Bethany Arts Community and Sundress Academy for the Arts. I'm indebted, too, to the wonderful people I wrote with in those places, especially to Maggie Foster and Bryan Parys—*oof!*—who crawled into my brain those weeks amongst the sheep!

Deep, deep gratitude to Anne Pollard James, who I've admired from afar since high school, and now get to admire much more closely, whose *Pretty Mouth* serves as the most perfect cover art I can imagine.

Thanks so much to Lauren Camp, Sean Singer, and Jessica L. Walsh for their endorsements, as well as to Patricia Spears Jones for her friendship, counsel, and encouragement. And, too, to Diane Lockward for believing in *This Strange Garment*.

Immense thanks to those who took care of me during my illness by driving me to appointments, making me bone broth soup, sitting masked by my convalescent bed, carrying string cheese up multiple flights of stairs, walking sweet Dolly, sending in cleaners, and adorning the house in flowers so huge as to make pain bearable: Addie Jones, Erryn Jones, Austin Kelley, Emily Thompson, Olivia Birdsall, Moira Donegan, Cleyvis Natera, and Jeannie Im. Thank you to my dear friend, Matt Nicholas, for carrying me candies across state lines and teaching me there is no "k" in Ziploc. Thank you to my health care team at Mt. Sinai Cancer Center in New York City: Dr. Natalie Berger, Dr. Sarah Cate, Dr. Jordan Jacobs, and the many staff, including Cliff and Vlad; also to Marnie Rustemeyer, the tattoo artist of my areolae. Thank you to my compassionate colleagues in New York University's Expository Writing Program, especially Jenni Quilter, Denice Martone, Richard Larson, Nate Mickelson, and Abby Rabinowitz, and to the university itself where my full-time faculty benefits provided me with both the time and care I needed.

Thank you to my family: my mother, Mary Thompson, who is singular in her presence and passion; my dad, Richard Hefner, and stepmother, Linda Hefner, who are a portrait of love and care; my stepfather, Thorn Huffman, who is as steady as they come. And finally, immeasurable thanks to my daughters, Eva and Ella, who gift me joy, peace, and wisdom every single day, and to my husband, Cody, who—in sickness and in health—allows me the space I need to love and write and be.

About the Author

Nicole Callihan is the author of *SuperLoop,* a full-length poetry collection, and five chapbooks, including *A Study in Spring* (with Zoë Ryder White), and *The Deeply Flawed Human*. She is also the author of the novella, *The Couples*. Her work has appeared in *American Poetry Review, Tin House, Kenyon Review, Colorado Review, Conduit,* and as a Poem-a-Day selection from the Academy of American Poets. A frequent collaborator with artists and composers around the world, her work has been translated into Spanish, German, Arabic, and Russian. She taught in New York University's Expository Writing Program for twenty years and now hosts both informal and formal poetry gatherings. She lives in New York City.

CPSIA information can be obtained
at www.ICGtesting.com
Printed in the USA
BVHW031207210223
658919BV00008B/145